BULL SHARKS

TAMMY KENNINGTON

Published in the United States of America by Cherry Lake Publishing
Ann Arbor, Michigan
www.cherrylakepublishing.com

Consultants: Dominique A. Didier, PhD, Associate Professor, Department of Biology, Millersville University;
Marla Conn, ReadAbility, Inc.
Editorial direction: Red Line Editorial
Book design and illustration: Sleeping Bear Press

Photo Credits: A Cotton Photo/Shutterstock Images, cover, 1; iStockphoto/Thinkstock, 5, 9, 11, 15, 21, 22;
Sleeping Bear Press, 7; Colin Newman/Dorling Kindersley, 13; Willyam Bradberry/Shutterstock Images,
17; Fiona Ayerst/iStockphoto, 18; Shutterstock Images, 19; Rainer von Brandis/iStockphoto, 25; Mayra
Beltran/Corpus Christi Caller Times/AP Images, 26; Shane Gross/Shutterstock Images, 28

Library of Congress Cataloging-in-Publication Data

Kennington, Tammy.
  Bull sharks / Tammy Kennington.
    p. cm. — (Exploring our oceans)
  Audience: 008.
  Audience: Grades 4 to 6.
  Includes index.
  ISBN 978-1-62431-405-6 (hardcover) — ISBN 978-1-62431-481-0 (pbk.) — ISBN 978-1-62431-443-8 (pdf)
  — ISBN 978-1-62431-519-0 (ebook)
  1. Bull shark—Juvenile literature. I. Title.

  QL638.95.C3K46 2014
  597.3'4—dc23   2013008484

Cherry Lake Publishing would like to acknowledge the work of
The Partnership for 21st Century Skills. Please visit *www.p21.org*
for more information.

Printed in the United States of America
Corporate Graphics Inc.
July 2013
CLFA11

ABOUT THE AUTHOR

Tammy Kennington holds a bachelor of arts in elementary education and is a certified reading
intervention specialist. She currently serves as a preschool director. Tammy lives in Colorado
Springs, Colorado, with her husband and four children.

TABLE OF CONTENTS

CHAPTER 1

PIT BULL OF THE OCEAN

The hook is baited. The line is cast. The team of Australian scientists looks into the water of the Brisbane River. They wait eagerly for the first catch of the day. The sudden tug on the line creates excitement as a researcher reels in his catch. He doesn't snag a catfish as he thought he would. Instead he pulls a young bull shark into the boat. It is not an odd event. Bull sharks can live in rivers all around the world.

The researcher needs to handle the bull shark with care. The bull shark is one of the three most dangerous

The bull shark can be found in rivers around the world.

LOOK AGAIN

WHAT DOES THE PHOTO REVEAL ABOUT THE BULL SHARK'S **HABITAT**?

sharks in the world. It is named in part after the land mammal of the same name. This is due to its **aggressive** behavior and broad, short snout. It has been called "the pit bull of the ocean." The bull shark is much smaller than the great white shark. Yet some scientists consider the bull shark the most dangerous ocean predator to people. This is because it enjoys the same ocean, lake, and river environments people do. The bull shark usually leaves humans alone in spite of its bad reputation. Still, people should be cautious when in the habitat of the bull shark.

Bull sharks favor shallow, warm waters. They lurk along the ocean's shoreline and swim through murky bays. The bull shark typically swims at depths of 3 to 450 feet (0.9–137 m). These are also the preferred depths of families splashing in coastline waters and of divers. The bull shark's range extends from Massachusetts to the Gulf of Mexico. It is also found around Latin America, Brazil, Australia, Indonesia, and the eastern Pacific Ocean.

RANGE MAP

RANGE OF BULL SHARK

ARCTIC OCEAN

North America

Europe

Asia

ATLANTIC OCEAN

PACIFIC OCEAN

Africa

South America

INDIAN OCEAN

PACIFIC OCEAN

Australia

Bull sharks do not live in deep, open oceans.

The bull shark is one of only six sharks known to live in both salt water and freshwater. It can live in a variety of habitats. These include warm coastal bays, **estuaries**, rivers, and lakes. Bull sharks have swum as far as 2,200 miles (3,541 km) into rivers such as the Amazon in South America and the Mississippi in the United States. Bull sharks have been found in Lake Nicaragua in Nicaragua, Central America. The bull shark has found access to the lake through rivers that feed into it.

The bull shark has more **testosterone** than any other animal on the planet. The shark is very protective of its territory. The bull shark is not the monster it is usually described as. But the bull shark is an animal to be treated with caution and respect. ◢

Bull sharks are dangerous predators, and people must be careful when in or near their habitats.

THICK AND GRAY

The bull shark is easily spotted by its thick, gray body. The shark also has a blunt nose that is broader than it is long. The bull shark has small eyes. This fact may point to the shark having less of a need for clear vision in murky waters. The bull shark has two dorsal fins. The first is large and triangular. The second is near the end of the body and much smaller. The dorsal fins help the shark keep its balance and keep it from tipping to the side. The tail fin shifts from side to side and helps the shark move forward. People may mistake the bull

LOOK AGAIN

LOOK CLOSELY AT THIS PHOTOGRAPH. WHAT SURPRISES YOU ABOUT THE BULL SHARK IN THIS IMAGE?

shark for the great white shark because the two sharks' fins look a lot alike.

The bull shark's gray and white **countershading** helps it hide from prey. Seen from above, the darker tone of the upper body blends in with darker water beneath the shark. Seen from below, the white belly blends well with the lighter, shallow water. Some young bull sharks have darker shading on their fins. This fades as they age.

Like other sharks, the bull shark's skeleton is made of **cartilage** instead of bone. Cartilage is a sturdy, flexible material. Bones weigh almost two times more than cartilage. A bony skeleton would require the bull shark to work much harder just to swim. The bull shark is one of only three sharks that has extra layers of calcium salts surrounding the cartilage in the jaw and spinal areas. (The great white shark and tiger shark also have these layers.) This helps give the shark even more strength in these areas.

Like other sharks, the bull shark's skin is formed from **dermal denticles**. These are tiny tooth-like scales. The dermal denticles create a rough texture similar to sandpaper. They provide strong, flexible protection. The scales of a bony fish increase in size as the fish grows, but dermal denticles remain small. Instead, more scales are made as the shark gets older. The shape of the dermal denticles lets the shark glide more easily through the water. This allows the shark to speed up quickly. The shark normally swims at a slow speed. But it has bursts of speed of 11 miles per hour (17.7 kmph).

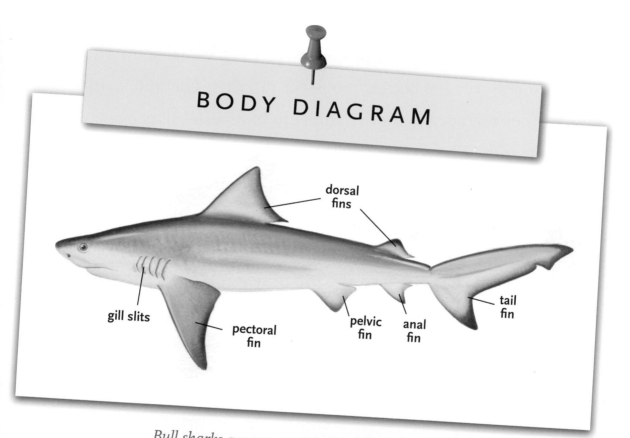

BODY DIAGRAM

dorsal
fins

gill slits

pectoral
fin

pelvic
fin

anal
fin

tail
fin

Bull sharks are gray on top and have blunt snouts.

Bull sharks have noses. But they only use them for smelling, not breathing. A bull shark breathes like other fish. Water enters the shark's mouth and moves back toward its gills. These organs pull oxygen from the water. Then, the oxygen travels through the rest of the body. The water exits the body through the gill slits. The bull shark does not need to move in order to have water pass over its gills. The shark can breathe by pumping water over its gills as well. Some researchers think this may be linked to the bull shark's ability to move from one habitat to another. Researchers continue to study this.

Most sharks are able to live only in salt water. But bull sharks can live in freshwater and salt water. This means they can remove salts from their bodies and retain water while in salt water. When the bull shark moves to freshwater, it keeps salts in its body and removes extra water. This process allows the bull shark to move from salt water to freshwater while keeping the right amount of salt and water in its body.

Bull sharks have thick bodies.

The bull shark's teeth may be its most powerful tool. The shark has 350 **serrated** teeth arranged in 50 rows. The shark is set to tear prey into large chunks for easier eating. When one tooth is damaged or lost another moves forward into its place. A bull shark has large teeth for its size. It also has the most powerful jaw of any large shark species. It is even more powerful than the great white shark's jaw.

Hunting and Eating

Imagine a bull shark swimming slowly through the water. It suddenly notices movement and speeds forward. Wham! The bull shark slams into its prey and circles back around. It moves toward its stunned victim and chomps down. Its razor-sharp teeth leave crescent-shaped bites.

The bull shark is heavy for its size and usually moves quite slowly. But it can have short bursts of speed to catch prey. The bull shark is also able to surprise larger, faster prey by using this "bump and bite" method. It has poorer vision than many other sharks. This method is a way for the shark to learn the strength and size of its target.

A bull shark uses its strong jaw to sink its large, sharp teeth into prey.

The bull shark uses its incredible senses to hunt for and catch prey.

The bull shark has a keen sense of smell. It uses that sense during hunting. It also uses **electroreception**. Electroreception is considered a shark's sixth sense. It is a shark's ability to detect an animal's electrical signals. Even creatures at rest or those hidden beneath sand or rocks give off electrical signals. Organs called ampullae of Lorenzini are located on the shark's snout. These detect electrical signals of prey in the water. Then they send messages to the shark's brain. This unique trait provides the bull shark with a lot of information about possible food sources.

The bull shark is a fierce predator, even at a young age. It prefers hunting alone. The many environments of the bull shark make good hunting grounds. The bull shark can choose from many creatures because it swims close

Bull sharks sometimes hunt in schools of fish.

to the shoreline where many animals live. The shark's favorite ocean foods include fish, dolphins, sea turtles, and even other sharks. Its freshwater menu includes mackerel, tarpon, and other fish that travel in schools. The bull shark is willing to eat almost anything. It has been known to take a bite out of dogs, horses, and cows that have waded into its habitat.

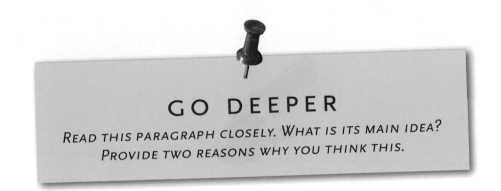

GO DEEPER

READ THIS PARAGRAPH CLOSELY. WHAT IS ITS MAIN IDEA? PROVIDE TWO REASONS WHY YOU THINK THIS.

CHAPTER 4

PUPS

Bull sharks can **mate** at any time of the year in tropical waters. But they usually mate only during the warm summer months. Most mating occurs where freshwater and salt water meet. Many bull sharks mate in the Gulf of Mexico.

The female shark is pregnant for ten to 11 months. Then she gives birth to one to 13 live **pups**. This is a small litter compared to many other shark species. The female will swim into a nursery before giving birth. This practice keeps pups safe from larger predators.

Tiger sharks, sandbar sharks, and larger bull sharks may try to eat young pups. The nurseries also offer shelter to the pups when the oceans are rough. These places also provide a lot of food for the hungry young sharks.

Mothers travel to safe nurseries before giving birth to their young.

The mother leaves her pups right after giving birth. The pups are able to hunt and protect themselves right away. They are between 2 and 3 feet (0.6–0.9 m) long at birth. As soon as they are born, the pups swim freely in their nursery. Bull shark nurseries have been found in Lake Pontchartrain, Louisiana, the Indian River Lagoon in Florida, and the Breede River in Africa.

Few bull sharks live past 20 years old.

Newborn pups grow quite quickly. They can grow up to 11 inches (28 cm) in their first year. Bull sharks are full grown when they are five to seven years old and 5 to 7 feet (1.5–2.1 m) long. Young bull sharks leave the nurseries at this time and live alone. Bull sharks seem to like their own space. Once they live alone, they avoid one another except when they mate. Mating starts when bull sharks are between eight and ten years old.

The average life span of a female bull shark is about 16 years. Males live to only about 12 years old. Some bull sharks have lived as long as 23 years.

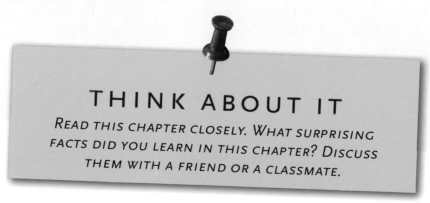

THINK ABOUT IT

READ THIS CHAPTER CLOSELY. WHAT SURPRISING FACTS DID YOU LEARN IN THIS CHAPTER? DISCUSS THEM WITH A FRIEND OR A CLASSMATE.

THREATS

Bull sharks have short life spans and small litter sizes. But there are still many of them in most coastal regions worldwide. One reason for this is because the shark is at or near the top of the food chain. The bull shark is an **apex** predator. The bull shark has few natural enemies as an adult. A tiger shark or a courageous crocodile may attack it.

The greatest threat to bull sharks is humans. **Fisheries** frequently catch bull sharks. Bull sharks are caught for their liver oil, skin, meat, and fins. A bull shark's liver oil

The bull shark has few natural enemies in its habitats.

Sportfishing is another threat to bull sharks.

is used to make lipsticks and face creams in the United States. The liver oil is used in other areas around the world too. The French use it to make cosmetics and perfume. People in India use liver oil to paint boats. Korea has one of the highest demands for shark liver oil. Koreans use the product in pills and medicines made for humans.

A bull shark's skin can be tanned and used as a leather product. Bull shark meat is frequently sold fresh, frozen, or smoked. Bull sharks are often more valued for their fins than for their liver oil, skin, or meat. The fins are the main ingredient in shark fin soup. It is a popular dish served in many Asian countries and in the United States.

The International Union for Conservation of Nature (IUCN) lists the bull shark as Near Threatened. This means bull sharks are in danger of having a limited population. More and more people live near where bull

Researchers continue to study
bull sharks in their natural
habitats and in captivity.

LOOK AGAIN
WHAT DO YOU THINK RESEARCHERS STUDY
WHEN THEY DIVE WITH BULL SHARKS?

[21ST CENTURY SKILLS LIBRARY]

sharks live. This can change the sharks' habitats. Pollution also creates risks to the population. The bull shark may soon be listed as threatened. But no laws are currently in place to protect the bull shark. Groups like the IUCN are working to pass laws that will limit bull shark sportfishing around the world. These groups also teach the public about the importance of bull sharks in the ocean.

Bull sharks are one of few shark species to survive in captivity for long periods of time. This allows researchers to study the incredible bull shark. Researchers hope to discover more about this powerful fish. They hope they will learn how to protect the species and help it live long into the future. ◢

THINK ABOUT IT

▲ Read Chapter 1 again. Compare and contrast the similarities and differences of the bull shark's different habitats.

▲ What was the most interesting fact you learned about bull sharks? What else would you like to know? Visit the library and choose another book about bull sharks. How does the information compare to what you have already learned?

▲ Review Chapter 3. What is the main idea? Summarize two or three details that support the main idea.

▲ In Chapter 5, you read the bull shark is listed as a Near Threatened species. Do you think it is important to protect the bull shark? Why or why not?

LEARN MORE

FURTHER READING

MacQuitty, Miranda. *Shark*. New York: DK, 2011.

Marsico, Katie. *Sharks*. New York: Scholastic, 2011.

Parker, Steve. 100 *Facts on Sharks*. Thaxted, UK: Miles Kelly, 2010.

WEB SITES

Discovery Kids—Sharks
http://kids.discovery.com/gaming/shark-week

This Web site lets readers learn about shark attack survivals and play games.

National Geographic—Sharks
http://animals.nationalgeographic.com/animals/sharks

Readers discover different species of sharks, learn more about the ocean, and play games at this Web site.

GLOSSARY

aggressive (uh-GREH-siv) showing violent behavior

apex (AY-pex) at the very top

cartilage (KAHR-tuh-lij) a hard, flexible tissue that forms certain parts of animals' bodies, such as a human ear or a shark's skeleton

countershading (KOUN-tur-shay-ding) the light and dark coloring of an animal to help it blend into its surroundings

dermal denticle (DUR-mul DEN-ti-kuhl) a sharp, tooth-like piece, such as the scale of a shark

electroreception (i-lek-tro-ri-SEP-shuhn) a type of sense that allows sharks to detect the heartbeats of their prey

estuary (ES-choo-er-ee) the wide part of a river, where it meets the ocean

fishery (FISH-ur-ee) the industry of catching, processing, and selling fish

habitat (HAB-i-tat) the place where an animal or plant usually lives

mate (MATE) to join together to produce babies

pup (PUP) a baby shark

serrated (SER-ay-tid) looking like the blade of a saw

testosterone (tes-TOS-tu-rown) a hormone that helps in the development of male traits

INDEX